Table of Conter

MW01193899

1 INTRODUCTION ....

Understanding laziness 2

2 KNOW IT, KILL IT 7

A habit like any other 7

3 SETTING PRIORITIES 13

The urgent vs. the important 13

4 MORE ON PRIORITIZING 18

Your key to productivity 18

5 STARTING YOUR DAY RIGHT 24

Enhance productivity one day at a time........................24

6 REPLACING OLD HABITS 30

Discipline yourself to get energized 30

7 PRACTICE MAKES PERFECT 37

Imbibing productive habits...37

8 WILLPOWER, DISCIPLINE, SELF-CONTROL 45

Developing mental strength..45

9 CONCLUSION 52

From sloth to super productivity....................................52

ABOUT THE AUTHOR 54

1 INTRODUCTION

Understanding laziness

Hard work might pay off later.
Laziness pays off now.

T-shirt line

A man was sleeping under a tree. A businessman happened to pass by.

"Hey you," he woke up the sleeping man. "Why don't you do some work instead of sleeping like this?"

"Why should I work?" Asked the man, rubbing his eyes.

"Why? To earn money," came the answer.

"And why should I earn money?"

"To enjoy life."

"Well, that's precisely what I'm doing," said the man and went back to sleep.

Let's face it: There's something intrinsically attractive about laziness. Given an option, very few want to get up and do something. It's why beanbags are popular, and so are pizzas and fast food. There seems to be a joy in just lazing around, without moving an inch or a finger. Any wonder Sundays are so precious?

Looked at it one way – and the lazy folks are going to love this – we humans were not meant to work. Look at animals in the wild. None of them work, or need to. Before man entered the picture and spoilt it for everyone, physical activity just to stay alive was unheard of. It's only us, especially in a modern setting, that need to get on the conveyor belt of work and keep walking to stay in the same place. We're hopelessly part of the rat race, and that means we need to keep working to live for a larger part of our existence.

Civilization has prepared us, very kindly, for a life of work. Little babies start working – under the guise of learning – when they are barely two. Then come many years of study (read: more work) till they graduate. Then they get ready for real work, in offices, factories and farms. Then they retire, at an appropriate age, and spend the rest of their days enjoying the fruits of their working life, or in penury. If it's the latter, they would be forced to do more work in their twilight years. As you can see, work is an inherent, inseparable part of life. And there's no escaping it.

With things the way they are, it makes eminent sense to prepare ourselves for work, rather than revolt against it. It's prudent, then, to reconcile with the factor called 'work' – if we can somehow learn to love it, the journey gets that much more enjoyable. And that's where this condition called 'laziness' comes in.

What is laziness – and why do we fall for it?

Well, we all know the definition. Any dictionary tells you that it's 'the quality of being unwilling to work or use energy'. It's a state of idleness or limbo when nothing happens. The best among us fall prey to this state of inaction – and it's natural.

The reasons behind laziness are several, but the most common are:

Lack of motivation
"Find purpose," said Mahatma Gandhi, "the means will follow." It's when you don't have a goal that you end up doing nothing – or waste time on meaningless stuff. Have an aim or objective, and that will help you stay motivated. Further on in this book, we'll give you more information on how to keep your motivation levels high.

Low energy levels
This could be physical or mental. "The spirit is willing, but the flesh is weak," says the Bible. Low energy levels can be tackled through vitamin and mineral supplements that help your body listen to your mind. If you feel tired all the time, maybe it's some exercise that you need. It's possible that you need to shed some weight to feel less sluggish. In any case, you need to feel agile and be active to get any work done.

The advent of technology
Believe it or not, technology makes us lazy – mentally and physically. There was a time, eons ago, when people knew mental calculation, then the adding machine came. People used to remember phone numbers, then came the mobile phone. Today, rather than touch just once, you ask Siri to call someone, while washing machines and dishwashers have made us physically lazy in the name of convenience. Not to say that technology is to be avoided and we need to do thankless chores; in fact technology can be used to promote productivity. Read on to know how.

Then there are all those reasons ("Today I'm not in the mood" or "I just don't feel like it") but most of them can be traced back to one of the above. And there seem to be as many causes for being lazy as there are people, which is why we need to make an important announcement before we go any further.

This book is less about symptoms and more about solutions. No point dwelling on the causes when we should be discussing the effects. That is the reason why we talk about the causes of laziness only briefly here in the introduction. The rest of the book is dedicated to finding ways out of your indolent disposition.

As you'll see, there are almost as many solutions to laziness as there are causes. But one man's meat is another's poison, so what works for one may not work for another. Go through the list and choose what works for you.

Is your commitment for real?

There's only one thing this book asks of you – commitment to cure yourself of your laziness. We'll be with you on this trip, handholding you every step of the way, coaching you on how to get rid of the malaise forever. That's our commitment.

But we need a similar commitment from you. To read this book, study the solutions and internalize them. Then you need to practice them, till you become perfect, because that's the only way you become less lazy and more productive.

To make it possible, we're being pragmatic about the contents of this book. You'll get less theory, and more practice. Less lecture, more action. Less of yarn and yawn, more of tips and tricks. Each of which you can put to use in your day-to-day life and see the results for yourself.

A word of caution though: Progress might be slow in the beginning. Old habits die hard and new ones are tough to implement. But don't lose heart. We're with you and, together, we can rid you of your laziness habit.

And by the way, don't be too lazy to go on. We need you to take small, baby steps and keep walking till you're ready and prepared to take giant leaps. Because, as the wise Chinese say, the longest journey begins with a single step. Let's take that one step now: Go to the next chapter.

2 KNOW IT, KILL IT
A habit like any other

A year from now,
you may wish you had started today.

Karen Lamb

Picture this: You're faced with a tub full of clothes that need to be ironed – one of the most boring jobs. What do you do? You put it away and reach for the remote. It's not as if something interesting is on the tube. Just that you've found an alternative to the least interesting task.

Another day, another time. You need to go to the dentist, about that cavity that's been troubling you for long. Clearly an unpleasant chore. It does pain you frequently, and it's unbearable, but right now it's dormant. Why bother about it and spoil a great evening? And what's the great evening all about? Wander aimlessly on social networks and feel bad about how well others are doing!

What's happening here? Look closely and you'll see what's common to these two scenarios: A distinct unwillingness to confront reality. You just want to shirk from what you need to do. Instead, you escape into familiar territory – mostly something worthless – and the time is gone, wasted.

When this sequence of events plays out a few times, your mind has detected a pattern. This is how habits form and let's understand: Laziness is a habit, and an undesirable one at that. And like with all habits, once entrenched into your system, it's tough to get rid of.

We humans can't exist in a vacuum. We're creatures of habit and our habits are what define us. Psychologists say that habits can be removed by the root only if they are replaced first. So you have people trying to kick the smoking habit by switching to electronic cigarettes, or munching bubble gum – a new, better habit replacing the old, bad one.

Same with laziness. Only thing, being humungous by nature, this one can't be overthrown by one single counter-habit but requires many sub-sets of habits. These, when introduced one by one at the right periods of time, can completely free you from the malaise of indolence.

But we've spoken enough. Now it's time for action. Here are six ways you can make a small difference to your life right now. Have a look and see which of them can be implemented as soon as you've read them.

Six tips to get you going

1. Create a list
Sometimes an avalanche of work hits you and the sheer force of it reduces you to inaction, rendering you lazy. Pick up a piece of paper and list out all the jobs that you need to do. A good list is half the battle won – because looking at it, you would get a bird's eye view of the situation. You'll now begin to feel that it isn't as bad as you thought, after all.

Next, prioritize the jobs from the list. Prioritizing is a large canvas in itself, meriting an entire chapter. You'll come to it soon. Also think: How many of the jobs do you need to do yourself – are there items on the list that you can delegate? Or maybe some of them could wait? This list clears the air and you'll now be able to do the easier tasks first and dwell on the more difficult ones later.

2. Start small

Let's say you have three things to be done and they've been weighing on your mind lately. You don't know what to do or where to begin. Here's the tip: Start with the smallest task of the three. Don't worry about the other two. Focus only on this task, concentrate on it, put all your energies in finishing it.

Once you've accomplished the task, you will be a different person. Not the demotivated individual with a defeatist attitude. By then, you would've broken your inner resistance and be willing to go for the next job.

3. From complex to simple

The biggest project would invariably be made up of many smaller components. You may have a thousand-page novel to write but you'll be writing only one page at a time. Break it down further and you'll realize that you write only one paragraph, one sentence, or even one word at any given moment. It's the magic of the task that hundreds of such tiny components make up your gigantic masterpiece.

It's the same with any large project. Take a sledgehammer and break the task down into as many pieces as possible. Study their degrees of difficulty, pick the simplest of the sub-tasks and begin. Being simpler, these sub-tasks can be easily done and get over rather quickly. And with each mini-achievement, you will be on a roll and be motivated to move on to higher sub-tasks. This way, the pressure of a huge deadline will cease bothering you and – like a mouse gnawing away at a mountain – you can complete the entire task relaxed and unhurried. (We have a huge tip on gnawing, read on.)

4. De-clutter your workstation

Often, when you set out to work, there are several things vying for your attention. Remove all such distractions from your desk by de-cluttering it. Keep only the things that you need for the immediate task. And not just physical objects like the remote or your mobile phone – even unwanted tabs in your browser can take you away from work. Close down all sites not connected to your work. These are precisely the escape routes you look for when you should be working. And these are the temptations and end up making you lazy. (More on this later.)

5. See yourself winning

As any psychiatrist can tell you, one of the secrets of success is to 'visualize' yourself succeeding. It's the same with work. Close your eyes and imagine you finishing the task at hand. Envision yourself as this enthusiastic person who's a fast worker, who finishes all jobs on time, and who earns the superior's praise. Think of the benefits of accomplishing the task – a public appreciation, or even a promotion.

Now open your eyes slowly. You'll experience a surge of energy that motivates you to start work. Don't lose that streak of energy – hold on to it and ride its wave. And like always, once you've begun, there would be no stopping you. You'll surprise yourself by attacking one task after another, and soon your job list would be empty.

6. Give yourself a pat on the back

You've done a great job, so now's the time to give yourself a reward. It doesn't need to be anything huge – even a bar of chocolate could do the trick. The idea is twofold: One, incentivize yourself with instant gratification so that you look forward to it in the future as well. And two, induce positive feelings in you linking them to your accomplishments. Just make sure you don't reward yourself *before* the task is fully complete. And that the reward is commensurate with the size of the task. If you've cracked a major presentation that could win your company a new client, chuck a toffee and treat yourself to a dinner at a fine dining restaurant.

So there, you have six little tips to try out. Of course, all of them test you – your willpower, discipline and self-control. After all, we're trying to dislodge a dangerous character trait here – it takes *some* effort. But it rewards you in ample measure too. Whatever works for you, keep at it, practice it to perfection. More on the way.

SOLUTIONS SNAPSHOT
What we learnt in this chapter

Laziness is a habit like any other.
To conquer it you need to replace it with other good habits, like discipline.
Six tips to begin with:
1. Develop a list of jobs to accomplish.
2. Start with smaller tasks, follow up with bigger ones.
3. Do simple jobs first, keep complex ones for later.
4. De-clutter your work area, remove all distractions.
5. Visualize yourself as completing your work, and earning accolades.
6. Reward yourself for every job accomplished.

3 SETTING PRIORITIES

The urgent vs. the important

*The key is not to prioritize
what's on your schedule,
but to schedule your priorities.*

Stephen Covey

Often, in an average day at work, you'll be inundated with tons of priorities. It's as if the floodgates have been opened and you've nowhere to hide. A situation like this can daze you into numbness, leading to zero action and no productivity. Could this be laziness of another kind?

Well, it needs tremendous amounts of willpower and self-control to get out of this conundrum and show results. Research indicates that not setting priorities is one of the seven reasons why people fail. So suddenly you're told that everything is priority #1. How to prioritize a set of super urgent jobs?

First, understand that when everything is a priority, nothing is a priority. If a song has the same pitch throughout and the same intonation, it's not a melody – it's just noise. The highs and lows of importance on a list is an indication of its priorities. Everyday firefighters at work understand that even when all tasks are 'urgent' some are more urgent than others.

Next, settle the now vs. later debate. Most people seem unable to determine if a job is urgent or merely important. And the difference is subtle but vast. Check it out:

Urgent: Demands immediate attention, mostly to do with say a superior's goals. Needs quick action as the consequences are immediate too. Tasks like phone calls, impending deadlines or quick response emails are also urgent things to do.

Important: Demands concentrated attention, but are not time-bound. Writing your novel is important but you can never finish it by evening. A startup company is important but it will take months.

The simplest example to illustrate this difference is a child throwing a tantrum – urgent – and that he needs to attend school regularly – important. It was Dwight Eisenhower who was quoted as saying in a 1954 speech: "I have two kinds of problems: The urgent and the important. The urgent are not important, and the important are never urgent." The Eisenhower Principle, as it came to be known, was used by the former US President to organize his priorities. Today executives employ it to prioritize their to-do list.

Third, are you just busy or are you also productive? Some people tell you, even as you enter the office, that they were up all night working on a project. But when you see what they've done you realize that the night had been wasted – at least the man could've caught up on his sleep! Are you checking your email often? Then it's a case of being busy without being productive. Better an hour's useful work than a whole day of dillydallying – it will only drain your energy to do any real work.

Now let's get down to some simple and sensible advice to help you set priorities.

Priority setting – tips and tricks

Where's your list?

It all begins with the list. When things get too mindboggling, bring out the paper and pencil. Even though you think you don't have a second to spare, and that the heavens are going to come down, take five minutes to sit down quietly in a secluded corner and jot down the various tasks for the day. Caution: Don't start prioritizing while you write the list. This will distract you and panic buttons will go off in your heart. Just write, fast and furious, and put in every job there is. You can always strike down the silly ones later.

Break your list down
Okay, so have all the jobs jotted down. Now categorize the jobs in two columns: short term and long term. So 'ironing clothes for the evening date' is short term, 'applying to music school' is long term. This gives you an idea of the matters that are truly pressing and matters that could wait a wee bit. You'll also see that long term tasks typically have many sub-tasks that can be tackled individually.

If your lists are too long, it might help to create several sub-lists. For example, you can have an indoor list for work to be done at home, and an outdoor list for work to be done outside. This way the lists get smaller, and you get a sense of order immediately, while motivated to finish one list after another.

Prioritize bigger tasks first – or is it the other way round?
Some people like to begin their day by tackling the major jobs, when your mind is fresh and can take bigger loads. The biggest jobs done are a huge relief; it's a joy to demolish the pyramid top down, and go for the smaller jobs later. For some others, the reverse works equally well. They need to get the high of finishing *something* first and then ride on that sense of accomplishment to attack the bigger tasks. Small jobs need less effort and can be finished quickly, so that's instant gratification. See which one works for you.

You may also look at the urgent-important comparison at the beginning of this chapter and prioritize accordingly. You might accord importance to your daughter's school project over your presentation, so be it. Or you might put off a trip to the mall to stay back and reply your emails. It's all up to you – as long as you're finishing stuff and your list is getting shorter by the hour.

Don't lose your list!
You may have done a wonderful job of listing out everything you need, and categorized and prioritized it – only to find out that your list is missing. If it's a home list, try sticking it on the refrigerator where you can also keep looking at it often. Or use Post-it notes at vantage points so that they catch your attention. If at work, you may open a stickie note or keep a desktop file that stares at you from the corner of the screen. All these remind you not to waste time and focus on the task at hand.

Feel the joy in ticking off jobs
There's no happiness equivalent to striking off completed jobs in a list. Experience it each time you tick off a task completed. Make it a celebration – at the end of the day, or when you take a break midway, go though the tasks already done and tick them off. This is your moment!

SOLUTIONS SNAPSHOT
What we learnt in this chapter

Prioritize, prioritize, prioritize.
Pick out the priority among priorities.
Distinguish between the urgent and the important.
Strive to be productive, not just busy.
Priority setting tips:
- Write down a list of tasks to be done.
- Categorize your list into short-term and long-term.
- Create sub-lists if needed, such as 'indoor' or 'outdoor'.
- Prioritize jobs as per size – start from the biggest or smallest.
- Preserve your list, and make it visible prominently.
- Experience the joy in striking down jobs from your list.

4 MORE ON PRIORITIZING

Your key to productivity

Lack of time is actually a lack of priorities.

Motivational poster

Prioritizing is your shortcut to getting more done, often in less time. When you prioritize, what you're essentially doing is cut out the riff-raff. It's the only way to know which jobs are critical and which aren't. Here are more tips on how to go about arranging your tasks in the order of importance.

Start with a good attitude

When you're going to hike a mountain, no point getting upset with a rock on the way. Be patient, you're in for the long haul. Work yourself into good humor and keep smiling – a happy mood only helps to get things done faster. Keep the big picture in mind and don't get perturbed if a few small things go wrong along the way.

How to whip up a good attitude? Smile, even if forcibly. With each smile, your body is releasing dopamine and endorphins that are known as feel good neurotransmitters. A smile also releases serotonin, an acknowledged mood enhancer. So keep smiling; you'll gradually notice that you're doing it more naturally.

Focus on the end result: Winning accolades having finished the task. Imagine your boss heaping praise on you. Visualize the cheers or envious looks of your colleagues. These images will motivate you to make a start, in the right spirit. A bad attitude is often the spark you need to put work aside, and you get sucked into the vicious procrastination cycle again.

Rank jobs as high, medium and low

Obviously some tasks are more important than others. Your kids' schoolwork or your office work that you brought home would be higher on the list compared to say, a social commitment or a household chore. Of course everything is relative and you need to understand what's important to *you*. Take your time marking tasks as H, M or L because any oversight in this exercise could turn your list topsy-turvy and your job list haywire.

Alternately, you could rank your tasks as difficult, easy and moderate – if that works for you. This harks back to the complexity of jobs discussed in the previous chapter, where we suggested starting with complex jobs or simple jobs as per your preference. A difficult-easy segregation tells you at a glance which ones are simpler to accomplish and perhaps you could begin with that list.

Compare lists, optimize workflow

Before you set off, you may want to quickly look at the plate in front of you. A comparison of lists will suggest ways on how you may want to attack the jobs. If a particular list looks attractive in terms of difficulty and time required, it may be a good idea to tackle it first.

On the other hand, if you have one humungous job that might require half the day – but will be a huge load off your head – it might make sense to just plunge into it first thing in the morning. With this big task out of the way, you'll feel a lot lighter to knock off the rest of the jobs post lunch. It'd also give you a kick in terms of achievement and you'd be better motivated to finish the rest.

Set reasonable deadlines

In your hurry to finish as many tasks as you can, you might allocate less time than a task might require. Give yourself between a half-hour and an hour for each job, depending on its nature. If you have a crazy day ahead and need to squeeze your exercise schedule in between, be judicious and restrict it to thirty minutes. On an easy day you can go the whole hog and do a one-hour workout.

Some tasks may need a few hours, so be tolerant. Be mentally prepared for sustained work, sometimes continuous. If you expect hardship, you'll be better attuned to handle it when it comes – if it does. More often, your worries could be false alarms that your mind has set up to prevent you from working.

Do one thing at a time, and do it well

Contrary to what multi-tasking champions tell you, doing many things at one time is not a good idea. Especially when you're bogged down by a backlog of jobs and are getting crushed under a heavy job list. The last thing you want is mixing up jobs and ruining your chances of getting something done.

There's just no way you can complete your job list by hopping from one task to another, doing a bit of this and a bit of that. You'll only end up with a hopelessly unfinished mess by evening. It's far more productive to finish them one by one – and your focused energies will ensure that it's done well.

That said, there's always the odd opportunity to combine tasks. For example, you can always review your physics notes while waiting at the Laundromat. There's no conflict between the tasks, both get done and you would've saved a considerable amount of time. All it takes is a bit of intelligent thinking – try it next time.

There are times when multi-tasking does work, or at least doing two jobs together. Of course, this is for the experts; you can try it too. See the following chapters for more.

Concentrate, focus on the finish line

Once you set a deadline and mentally agree that there's enough time to complete the task, there's no looking back. You're all set. Now nothing should deter you from starting the work and staying focused on doing it.

Concentration is the key. Strengthen your willpower and let your mind not get distracted. This is where your self-control and discipline come into play: Tell yourself that come what may, you'll not let go until the task is completed. Keep working uninterrupted; let no power come between you and the finish line.

Should you do everything yourself?

Not at all. As you go through your job list, you'll come across tasks that could be delegated. Of course some of them might need your expert touch, or some could be too big to be done by your little son. But there are bound to be jobs that are better off handled by others.

You'll also discover that some jobs needn't be done at all. In your enthusiasm you may have included them in your list, but now you realize that they aren't worth the trouble. If the drudgery is more, and the saving (time, money) is less, why bother? Be ruthless – strike them off the list at once!

Take breaks between tasks

What does a seasoned marathon runner do? He doesn't run the first hundred meters as if it's a sprint. He starts smart and steady, running fast yet conserving his energy, keeping an eye on his opponents, ready to run the final laps with speed when his rivals would be slowing down. That's his strategy.

Similarly, you need a strategy. When tackling long job lists, you need to prepare your mind for the marathon and keep it in good shape. So what do you do? Take frequent breaks. Give your mind tiny periods of rest, especially between two tasks. This way, you'll be on top of the job list.

You also need to keep your mind fresh without tiring it out beyond capacity – requiring you to categorize your job list intelligently. If you fatigue it out early and stress it over the remaining unfinished jobs, it would stop responding altogether and all your plans go kaput.

Another way to stay fresh is to choose different tasks to do. Never repeat a similar kind of job – for example, doing up the bed and laundry. Insert an unusual task in between two identical tasks. Go through your little girl's test results after vacuuming but before polishing the furniture. Alternating your jobs in this manner makes you less fatigued, and keeps your mind blooming.

On achieving a task, be easy on yourself

Let's say you've completed a mammoth job, or finished a series of smaller tasks. It's goodies time! Tell yourself you've done it – and give yourself a mental pat on the back. You could even give yourself a small treat, or switch on the television for a five-minute de-stressor break. Just make sure that the procrastination bug doesn't bite you and five minutes become fifty.

This is only meant to drive you on, so keep your reward short and sweet. It's okay to watch the rain for a while between your schoolwork, but it's not okay to get into bed, pull up the sheets and cozily go to sleep.

SOLUTIONS SNAPSHOT
What we learnt in this chapter

- Start positively. Work on yourself to begin with a good attitude.
- Ladder your jobs as high, medium and low.
- Match your job lists to get the best out of your workflow.
- Be practical when setting timelines.
- Focus on doing one thing at a time; it turns out well.
- When working, just work. No slacking off.
- Pepper your jobs with frequent, small breaks.
- As you complete tasks, treat yourself in small ways.

5 STARTING YOUR DAY RIGHT

Enhance productivity one day at a time

Each morning we are born again.
What we do today is what matters most.

Buddha

The alarm goes off. Your hand reaches for the snooze button. Just ten more minutes, you tell yourself. Then you hear the alarm again – and panic. You're going to have another crazy morning. You leap out of bed, dart into the shower, dart out, dress up in a jiffy, try to get some coffee, burn your tongue, and you're off. This routine, unfortunately, is on replay mode and unfolds every morning.

For most people, mornings aren't the favorite time of the day. The majority, quite simply, aren't 'morning persons'. Under the safe classification of being 'night persons' they play out this hurried charade five mornings a week.

Mornings are powerful

Like it or not, morning is the most powerful part of the day. Your morning sets the tone for the entire day to follow, so how you treat it determines what you get done till evening. Which is why if you want to have a productive day, have a productive morning – and if you want to change your life, you need to change your mornings.

Just what does a great morning offer? More energy, higher efficiency, clearer thoughts and a better attitude. It's all your need to navigate through the day and make it constructive. Not only will you feel better, you'll look better and will be brimming with confidence. How to achieve it? Read on.

A great morning begins the night before

Remember this cardinal principle: A morning is only as good as the night that preceded it. If you'd had a late night, your morning would be lousy with lack of sleep. If you'd had alcohol, you will be hung over. If you'd had inadequate shuteye, you will be carrying the rest of the sleep in your eyes through the day.

The trick is to retire early. Figure out how much sleep you need and make provision for it. No late night television or other distractions. Have a fixed time to get into bed and stick to it.

If you're unable to sleep, find out why. Read a book, walk around till you tire yourself out, keep a notebook to write down your concerns. Do something. Mostly, stop thinking. Remember what the Zen master says: 'When walking, walk. When eating, eat.' When sleeping, sleep – and not worry about a hundred things that happened or didn't during the day. Calm your mind and get it prepared to rest. Because the deeper you sleep, the fresher you feel on waking up.

Don't interrupt the morning

It's the snooze button that does. Avoid it like the plague. When the alarm goes off the first time, your body hears it and releases adrenaline – and you're alert. So when you hit the snooze button, you're asking the brain to stop being alert and go back to sleep. What happens? Your drift off again, with your brain starting its sleep cycle from the beginning. Now the alarm goes off again, and you're in the early part of your sleep cycle – you'll find it tougher to wake up now, feeling worse than before.

How to change this? Simple – turn the negative into a positive. Think of the alarm not as something that interrupts your sleep but as a wakeup call to new opportunities. But for your alarm, you'd waste your mornings snoring away in your bed while the world would be up and running. It's a brand new day, embrace it.

With practice, the alarm becomes your friend. It's part of the natural flow of your mornings and you'll be able to take its prompt and wake up.

Be an early riser

'Early to bed, early to rise, makes a man healthy, wealthy and wise.' It's not for nothing that our ancestors coined this golden phrase. Think: Has anything worthwhile been ever accomplished by anyone sleeping late into the morning? Every achiever, every entrepreneur in history, woke up early and began work well before sunrise. For them, early morning presented a time that was fresh and without interruptions, hence the best time for productivity. Some of them rise early and go for an early morning run. Some others work for an hour before their family wakes up. And still others wrap up quite a few tasks well into breakfast – the power breakfast – and are ready for the office.

Why mornings? For one, fewer distractions. Once you hit the office, you're likely to be swept by demands from all quarters. For another, your willpower is stronger early in the morning. As the day wears by, you get tired and your willpower gets worn out. Make the best use of it while it is at its most powerful. Also, a happy morning is a great beginning to the day, giving it a rush of positivity.

How to maximize your mornings

You may not be an entrepreneur with hundreds of things to attend to. But that doesn't mean you have nothing to do early in the morning. Plan your morning in the evening, invest in it wisely, and follow that schedule till it becomes a comfortable routine. Here are a few things to do after you rise and shine:

Be grateful for what you have
While this is great to remember any time of the day, it's especially good to start your morning with it. Look at all the good things in your life and send a silent thank you prayer to the power above. To quote David Steindl-Rast, "…it's not happiness that makes us grateful but gratefulness that makes us happy." Count your blessings.

Have a glass of water
It makes you alert and kick starts your metabolism, helping in weight loss. It also hydrates you, flushes out toxins, fires up your brain while also ensuring that you eat a little less. A glass of warm water with lemon is also a healthy habit – it gives you a dose of Vitamin C as well as cleanses your liver and kidneys.

Get some exercise
Begin in small doses – anything from walking, cycling, jogging, gym or yoga. Exercise helps you think clearly so you can think through and formulate your decisions ahead.

Set your goals for the day
Some prefer to do this the night before, while others like to do it in the shower or on their way to work. Either way, it gives you enough time to prepare mentally and plan in advance.

Sit and meditate
All you do is sit down on the floor in a comfortable corner of your room, close your eyes and think about nothing. Try to stop the incessant chatter in your head. Calm your mind, stay that way for five minutes. You can increase the duration gradually.

Give your brain a workout
When you read the newspaper, do the crossword. Or solve the Sudoku. If you're into scrabble, and have an online game going, make a few moves. Any of these will wake your brain up and get it charged right away.

Enjoy a great, healthy breakfast
You may have heard the axiom: 'Breakfast like a king, lunch like a commoner and dinner like a pauper.' It's perhaps the best advice on how – and how much – to eat. Your breakfast is the day's most important meal, so make it your healthiest. Eat slowly, chew well, and if needed, make the newspaper its accompaniment. Make sure that you consume less caffeine and perhaps a bowl of fresh fruit and yogurt. A healthy breakfast gives you the energy to concentrate better and be more productive, helps to maintain the right body weight, stops you from in-between snacking, and provides you with all the necessary nutrients, vitamins and minerals.

Get dressed – well
Take the effort and time required to look good – it's an important part of productivity. Dressing well helps you to look professional, build your confidence and testifies to the fact that you're a detail-oriented, organized individual. It's a well-known fact that when you look good, you perform better. Dress to impress, and you'll floor them in more ways than one.

According to psychologists, you're at your productive best within an hour of waking up, and for about two hours after that. This could be your most creative time, and you can't benefit from it if you're not prepared for it mentally and physically. Follow the routine given above – with such a regimen you'll forget all about laziness. Develop your willpower, consolidate your self-control and enhance your discipline levels. Be your best.

SOLUTIONS SNAPSHOT
What we learnt in this chapter

The importance of mornings – a day started well also ends well.
Prepare for the morning the night before.
Flow with the morning without interrupting it.
Early risers are achievers. Remember: The early bird catches the worm.
Put your early hours to good use:

- Count your blessings.
- Start your morning with a glass of water.
- Get a physical workout.
- Set your goals for the day.
- Get a mental workout.
- Eat a slow, healthy breakfast.
- Make the effort to look dapper.

6 REPLACING OLD HABITS

Discipline yourself to get energized

Action may not always bring happiness;
but there is no happiness without action.

Benjamin Disraeli

We've already seen that laziness is a habit. And like any habit, it has the ability to consume our lives. But the good news is that like any habit again, it could be gotten rid of.

Habits can seep into the psyche and entrench themselves deep. Which is why initially you'll not be able to remove them completely. You'll need to replace them with other, good habits. You'll then need to stay with the good habits, practicing them, till they get entrenched in place of the old ones.

In this chapter let's look at some new habits to discipline and motivate you.

New Habit #1: Bring order to your world

This could be the most important habit you'll inculcate in yourself, because often laziness originates from clutter and lack of clarity. A cluttered desk or crowded workstation can cause you to not initiate any work, or postpone it, or even abandon it altogether.

In contrast, an organized and clean workspace is very inviting. You will be drawn naturally to a well-arranged desk and, in spite of yourself, you'll sit and start working. This applies to the physical space around you as much as the space in your laptop – you need to arrange your files and make your computer inviting as well. And just like how you dump garbage into the bin, dump all unwanted or distracting files into the trash can.

Make it a habit to clean up your immediate surroundings frequently. Ensure that your workstation or desk is uncluttered and welcoming.

New Habit #2: Update your list – every night

We mentioned lists in the earlier chapters. If there's one discipline you can follow to uproot that laziness habit, it would be to write down the tasks to be done.

To make this exercise more effective, keep the list by the bedside. Before going to sleep, cross out jobs done and add jobs for the next day. Likewise, first thing in the morning, glance at your list of tasks. This helps you to be always on top of the work and to internalize the importance of accomplishment.

Better still, have a small pocketbook and carry it with you everywhere. As you get more disciplined, and start getting more things done, you'll discover that there are small windows of time that get free in between. With your pocketbook handy, you can jot down forgotten tasks or other ideas that can make you even more productive. You never know when an idea can strike – while driving, at the mall, in the elevator – and it'll be useful to not let them float away into oblivion.

New Habit #3: Be super conscious of time

By now you'll realize that time is the most critical factor in getting anything done, because work is always done in relation to time. And doing things on time is what separates laziness and productivity.

There are two things you need to do:

- Allocate the time required against each task and honor that time line.
- Keep small clocks at all vantage points around the house – in the kitchen, in the washroom, in the corridors.

When you imbibe time-consciousness 24/7, you'll be deeply aware of the seconds ticking by. In the back of your mind, you'll always be thinking of the work that's going on and the tasks that still need to be done. Clocks all over the house will help you in this exercise.

New Habit #4: Master the art of 'nibbling'

When confronted with a huge task, you're likely to be overwhelmed by its sheer size. Worry not – there's a simple way around it.

We already know that a big job is nothing but a combination of many small jobs. What you need to do is attack them one by one. But sometimes you'll notice that even the smaller components are big in themselves and you cannot break it down any further. This is where a technique called 'nibbling' can be put to excellent use.

You take a job and 'nibble' at it a little. Just like a mouse gnawing at the edge of a cookie, do a little of the task on the sidelines. Do it for five or ten minutes, leave it and do another job. Then say after an hour, revisit this big task and nibble at it a little more. Many such nibbles make a large bite and perhaps by the end of the day you'll realize that a sizable chunk of the job has been done.

Nibbling is effective against laziness too.

Let's say you're being plagued by plain old laziness – just no inclination to do anything. You need to get going with your willpower, but that isn't easy either. So what do you do? Put nibbling into action.

You're unable to wake up. Do a little nibbling: Tell yourself that you'll get up only for a minute, and that you'll go back to sleep after that. Use a tiny iota of willpower and get up – you'll be able to, because you're going right back to sleep after all. Then the magic happens: Once you're awake for one full minute, you'll feel less inclined to sleep again.

There are other ways to nibble to prevent you from hitting the bed again. For example, nibble at some odd jobs. Fold your sheets. Or glance at the newspaper headlines. Or look out the window for thirty seconds. Or just sit down, silently, for a whole minute. You'll notice that sleep has vanished from your eyes. You're more agile than you were a minute ago and not so keen to go back to bed.

Where else does nibbling work? Practically everywhere – in fact, this is one big idea that puts laziness out the door. Say you haven't hit the treadmill in months. And you just can't bring yourself around to turn that switch on. Nibble at it. Tell yourself that you'll only walk for two minutes, and stop even before the belt picks up speed. Keep walking for two minutes as planned. Chances are you'll hang on for a minute more, and another minute, and before you know it you've spend a full ten minutes on the treadmill. There, you've done your daily workout!

All these actions can be repeated the next day. Having done a ten-minute workout almost unconsciously, you will have discovered how effortless it can be. And you'll be more than willing to repeat the action. Thus the cycle goes on – and a good habit has taken root.

New Habit #5: Up your milestones

So there you are, right in earnest, working your ass off at meeting timelines. You've told yourself that you'd work for thirty minutes straight before taking a five-minute breather. That's great!

Now there's something you need to do. Up that milestone to forty-five minutes, and then take a break. Every few days, increase your work span by fifteen minutes and soon you'll see yourself working for hours straight. You'll increase your stamina for work and turn into a workaholic in no time.

Then again, becoming a workaholic isn't your goal. Your goal is to become a productive individual who can get things done, come what may. Who wants someone that's always thinking of work and forgets to live? Which is why the next new habit is very critical.

New Habit #6: Take rest frequently

We've understood the need to keep your mind fresh, and to take frequent breaks. If you've followed all the tips in the book and have turned into a changed individual, you deserve more. You deserve a whole day's rest.

Yes, we're talking about taking a break on Sunday. You haven't been lazy for a while, and it's a great feeling to be productive through the week. You're bound to feel like an achiever and you deserve to. But beware: If you overdo the work discipline, there's a real danger of burning out. And the backlash can be severe and sometimes irrevocable for a long time. It's like one step forward and two steps backward.

This can be prevented by taking your Sunday off. After all, the whole world is closed on that day and you can, without guilt, afford to hit the snooze button. Take it easy, ignore phone calls, don't answer emails. Just chill.

There's only one rider: Don't take Sunday into Monday. Leave it right there and when the clock strikes twelve, you shouldn't be awake but away in slumber land, sleeping at least past one hour. Remember that the fun of Sunday is greater when you willingly go back to your routine the next day onwards.

A good idea would be to gradually slide into work mode by Sunday late evening. Go back to your to-do list, open your pocket book, and see what's in store for you in the coming week. When you finally hit the bed, your head should be brimming with excitement at completing a new set of jobs. You would've already lined up the sequence of tasks, visualizing yourself completing them and earning praise. The most important day of the week – Monday – will arrive in a few hours, so sleep tight.

SOLUTIONS SNAPSHOT
What we learnt in this chapter

Laziness habits need to be replaced with productivity habits.
- New Habit #1: Organize your world.
- New Habit #2: Update your to-do list the night before. Keep a notebook for work ideas.
- New Habit #3: Be aware of time passing. Allot time for each task, and adhere to your timelines. Keep clocks everywhere and become a clock-watcher.
- New Habit #4: Practice 'the art of nibbling'. You can nibble at everything, from work to workouts.
- New Habit #5: Prolong your milestones to increase work stamina.
- New Habit #6: Take Sundays off – go back to your lazy self. It's the best way to rejuvenate yourself for the coming week.

7 PRACTICE MAKES PERFECT

Imbibing productive habits

*If today was the last day of my life,
would I want to do what I'm about to do today?*

Steve Jobs

That, in a nutshell, is what being productive is all about. If laziness is about doing nothing, productivity is about doing the right thing – not just anything. You can always keep working without knowing where you're going with it. But if you have clear objectives in mind, and a time frame to finish the task in, then we're talking.

But enough of mollycoddling. We've been soft on lazy folk so far, now no more of it. From this chapter on, we're moving from being defensive to being offensive. So far we've looked at ideas that prevent you from getting into the laziness habit. Now we up the ante – by doing the opposite. We now seize the initiative and give you habits that make you super productive.

To achieve that, like always, there are habits that you need to adopt and ingrain within yourself. These are the habits that turn passive employees into entrepreneurs, and small time businessmen into billionaires. And as before, you need to discipline yourself through self-control and create regimens that deliver success. Let's study them in detail.

What's the most productive part of your day?

Your workday is likely to be a rollercoaster of action – there would be crests in it as well as troughs. The same applies to the different parts of the day. For some, mornings are the best time to work, since they are fresh in their mind. For some others, evenings seem to work well, at the end of the day when all other work is done and everyone is gone. You need to figure out what's your best time of day.

Identify it and pack it with the most important jobs of yours. If you have a golden window of time where your faculties are at their peak, that's when you need to optimize it by getting your key tasks done. With practice, you'll start doing this automatically – but in the beginning when you're still finding your feet with productivity, you may have to consciously prioritize tasks to get the best results.

'Funnel' your tasks for the day

When you pencil in your to-do list, you'll automatically start placing the more important jobs on top. This kind of funneling ensures that the less important jobs get stacked at the bottom. It's a bit like how reporters write news items in newspapers. Since space is at a premium, they pack the top of the article with important facts so if they want to chop it they can easily do it at the bottom without any loss of information. Do the same with your job list.

Over time, you'll get used to listing the least important jobs towards the end. You'll also see the merit in focusing on 'make or break' tasks as compared to the deadwood.

Cut out the unwanted

As you progress with your to-do lists and march on completing your tasks, you'll see that some jobs aren't required to be done at all. Of course this happens only after you've evolved into an expert at job lists and how to tackle them.

Next time you're looking at your list and are about to take up a task, ask yourself: Is this job really important? If it's not, no point wasting time doing it. You're better off completing another task that makes a real difference to you.

What are those irritants again?

There you are, concentrating hard on the task at hand, and making steady progress. Suddenly it pops up on the right top of your computer screen, with an audio accompaniment: An email has arrived.

What's your first instinct? To go see it. Only after you click on it you'll know that it wasn't worth it. But what happened in the meanwhile? You broke the flow of work, your thread of thought snapped and your stream of enthusiasm has been curtailed. Your productivity has been hijacked.

When you sit down to do serious work, there are certain obstructions to work that you need to remove. This includes disabling desktop notifications to your mail, closing social networks, muting your mobile phone (or switching it off), turning off the music and anything else that acts as a speed-breaker to your progress.

This will ensure two things. One, you won't be tempted to connect to people when you're steeped in work. Two, you're not letting people connect with you while you're busy. Then, having insulated yourself from the distracting world temporarily, watch how smoothly your work moves ahead towards completion.

Never work non-stop

You're not a robot – nor should you become one. Work is a goal all right, but it's also a subset of a larger objective. So don't miss the wood for the trees.

Research studies have proven that working non-stop is counterproductive. On the other hand, when you take what are called 'strategic breaks', your productivity shoots up. Yes, you'll be spending more time working, but you'll get far less in terms of finished work. So you'll end up, as the Law of Diminishing Returns demonstrates, working more for getting less done.

However passionate you'll eventually get about work – and we hope you truly do – work isn't everything. Work will be a tremendous source of satisfaction and achievement but it's not a replacement for your family, health or emotions like love and affection. Hence the need to take strategic breaks.

What comprises a strategic break? It could be anything outside the scope of your vocation that qualifies as 'work' for you. For example, gardening may be 'work' for a gardener but for you it could be the number one de-stressor. When you take a hiatus in what you've been doing for hours, you're actually resting your mind and recharging it. Once it rejuvenates itself – either by being idle or occupying itself with other unrelated activities – your brain will be ready to race on turbo again.

Can 'work' be a break?

The super workaholics of the world are a whole different species. Do you think they ever stop working? Fat chance.

Instead, there's something that they do. They switch their 'work'. For example, if a man is a writer and painter, he could be writing for four hours and taking a break with painting. After that, he's more likely to go back to writing than be idle. Of course, for people like these productivity is never an issue. They do have their goals, but essentially it's the joy of the process that turns them on. The sheer act of working, of being busy, of attaining milestones big and small, the glory of completing an assignment – these are the driving force of their lives.

Talking of taking breaks with work, creative people find that doing two tasks simultaneously can be highly productive. They regularly alternate between one job and the other and end up excelling in both. What gives? When the mind is actively working on one task, it continues to work subconsciously on the other. So when you switch from the first to the second – bingo! – mind comes up with a ready solution for the latter. This kind of switching back and forth will eventually help both jobs and the person working stays fresh with no fatigue. Worth a try!

Nothing works? Walk away from it

Sometimes, in spite of doing everything possible, your mind just doesn't move. Nothing clicks inside it, no ideas or solutions pop up – curtailing the speed of your work. This could be a mental block, your mind refusing to work anymore in protest. Could be overwork, could be fatigue, but your brain has struck work. Now what?

First, don't panic. When you are full of nervous anxiety, your mind just freezes and then it might take days to unfreeze it. So – just stay put and let out a smile. Accept that such things happen, your mind is a living thing after all, you aren't a robot yet. It's a bit like what we do when our computer gets stuck – quite simply we reboot it. That's exactly what your mind needs.

How to give it a quick reboot? You obviously can't go to sleep at work, so short of that anything is allowed. One of the foremost things you can do is to 'walk away from it all'. Yes, literally and figuratively. Get up from your desk, go to a colleague's office and chat her up (if she's free). Go for a stroll in the corridor or on the lawn outside. Stop to smell the flowers (you haven't done that in a long while anyway). Look at the birds and bees and wonder at their lives sans projects and deadlines. Touch a leaf.

Then, casually, turn back. Stop by at the bathroom and freshen up. Talk and laugh with co-workers along the route. Walk via the coffee machine, pick up a cup. That will help you perk up even more. (Of course you shouldn't overdo the caffeine bit.) On returning to your desk, chances are, you would've whipped up your enthusiasm and prepared your mind to deliver again.

Make the best of your in-between times

Your day is littered with little pockets of time that often go unnoticed, and hence unutilized. You get five minutes walking to the metro station. You get twenty minutes in the metro. You get three minutes waiting for a meeting to begin. You get seven minutes walking from your office at one end to the boss's office at the other. Add up all those little windows and you get a large French window with an hour of extra time in a day. Make yours a 25-hour day!

Make no mistake, these in-between times can be used very productively. Make that call to your grocer walking to the metro station. Read that latest book on marketing on your train ride. Reply to a few emails while waiting for the meeting to start. Listen to that important podcast on your walks within the office. Each of these tasks would be resting on your to-do list, waiting for their hour under the sun. Now you've attended to all of them without disturbing your main schedule.

Equally important, you've made every second accountable. You're buzzing with activity, keeping your mind busy, and that puts the surge of energy in you – and you'll end up getting more work done.

If it's repetitive, it can be automated

With today's technology, you can be spared of doing chores that are regular and recurring. Which means you don't need to attend to them physically – you just need to 'set' them to be done automatically. When your computer can accomplish tasks on its own, as per your instructions, it's a shame that you still sit up late to do them.

- Mark emails you don't want as spam, so you needn't bother to delete them.
- Set up filters to direct your emails into different folders, so you don't have to sort them out and archive them physically.
- If social networks are too tempting for you, try these website blockers: *StayFocusd, LeechBlock, WasteNoTime.* They can block your access to websites for specified periods. Invaluable!
- Automate all your regular payments – easily done through standing instructions with your bank or your vendor. One headache off your list.

At the end of the day, you can choose to be busy or you can choose to be productive. With the first, you're always occupied, forever on the conveyor belt of life, always running to say in the same place. With the second, you work in such a way that there's a provision to play. Because, as the cliché goes, all work and no play makes you extremely dull indeed.

SOLUTIONS SNAPSHOT
What we learnt in this chapter

From being less lazy, take the giant step into hyper productivity.

- Identify the best part of your day for optimum work – best for your toughest tasks.
- 'Funnel' your jobs – top down from most important to least.
- Don't do tasks that are 'not important'. Chuck them!
- Remove obstructions to work – notifications, calls, text messages.
- Don't be a robot. Take 'strategic breaks' – distractions from your main work.
- Sometimes, 'other work' can be the break from your 'current work'. Explore this.
- If you hit a mental block, walk away from it – for a short while.
- Do small tasks in those 'in-between' times – while walking, waiting, commuting.
- Automate repetitive chores. Use that time for productive tasks instead.

8 WILLPOWER, DISCIPLINE, SELF-CONTROL

Developing mental strength

For a man to conquer himself
is the first and noblest of all victories.

Plato

If you've come so far in this book, you already know the importance of mental strength in defeating laziness. Every tip given till now, every piece of advice, links back to using your mental prowess to overcome sloth. The unfortunate part is that everyone wants to be productive and successful but very few want to invest in developing a strong mind – with which they can control their destinies.

What's mental strength? It's the ability of your mind to listen to you in the face of temptation or inaction. And it's a combination of your willpower and self-control, tempered by discipline. Indeed, the first two are almost synonyms of each other, while the third is the outcome. It can be safely said any one of them is incomplete without the other two.

Let's understand these attributes in detail.

Defining willpower

Willpower is considered as the ability to overcome instant pleasure, and resist temptation in the short term to achieve goals in the long term. Most of us have heard of the 'marshmallow experiment' in which a kid is left in a room with a single marshmallow for an hour. If he resists the temptation to eat it in that time, he gets two marshmallows later. Needless to say, more kids waited for the second marshmallow than settle for just one.

Strong willpower helps you to overpower feelings and emotions, while empowering you to ride over them through logic. Many individuals develop it consciously as a tool to regulate their actions. Psychologists argue that willpower is a limited resource, to be used carefully, though this premise hasn't been corroborated by research yet.

Willpower is the force that gives you self-control, with which you can avoid succumbing to momentary impulses. It empowers us to pause and think – so that you can look at optional responses. It also prevents you from jumping into things that could be regrettable later.

Scientifically speaking, willpower resides in the right brain in a section called prefrontal cortex. Willpower is known to use up glucose, causing depletion of the ego. When this happens, our reserves are low and our guard is down, and we tend to indulge and overeat. This explains why people going through stress tend to put on weight easily.

In layman's terms, willpower is the capability to do something even if you don't feel like doing it. Research studies have shown that kids who grow up with more self-control become adults who're stable and secure, not to mention scoring high in self-discipline. This, in turn, leads to better performance academically and happier lives. In fact, self-control is the one single contributor to the long-term success of an individual.

Willpower is like brainpower. Use it less and it weakens. Employ it more and more and it gets fitter and stronger. If you've always lived a life of surrender, it would be tough for you to develop willpower. Some psychologists also liken it to a muscle – neglect using it and it sags. Keep stretching it and it gets more resilient.

Needless to add, self-control is the key to overcome fears and obsessions, and to prevent unwelcome behavioral traits. When practiced well, it puts you in charge of your life, developing your tolerance and patience, improving your relationships, and enabling you to succeed repeatedly. It also empowers you to avoid excesses and attain moderation; assists you to control your moods and reject negativity; and strengthens your self-esteem and inner strength. Self-control helps you to become a complete, well-rounded personality.

But for willpower to work, you need to make it work – and you should be determined for it. Temptation appeals to the sub-conscious while willpower resides in the conscious, so you need to make constant, serious efforts to improve it. Here are few simple ways to add more muscle to your will.

Try to resist temptation at every opportunity

We've all heard the cliché: 'Where there's a will, there's a way.' Temptation is all around us – in different sizes, shapes and intensities. From enjoying a cake to watching a thriller, everything is temptation. When faced with one, attempt to ward it off. Tell your mind to fight it and immerse yourself in some other activity. It may not work the first time, or even the second, but gradually you'll gain the strength to fight it. Just say No and stay with your decision.

If at first you don't succeed, postpone

This works like magic. If you can't say No to the cake right away, tell yourself that you'll have it tomorrow. When tomorrow comes, say the same thing. Keep putting it off, and eventually you'll realize that you're not tempted by it anymore. This is because your mind can't accept No for an answer. But if you tell your mind that you can have it later, it agrees. Postpone temptation forever.

Point to remember: Don't tire your will by constant negation. If you constantly deny it the pleasure it's seeking, its edge gets blunted. Since willpower isn't considered to be infinite you've got to expend it with care. Hence the next point.

Remove all temptations from your vicinity

If cakes are your weakness don't store them in your refrigerator. Prevent temptations from entering your home, then there's no way you'll fall for them. If the television is a temptation, unplug it or – better still – disconnect the cable connection. Out of sight is out of mind, and you don't miss what you don't see (in most cases). Ensure that your immediate environment is free from such attractions; your willpower will thank you for it.

Equip your body to resist temptation

If you're serious about boosting your willpower, you need to get your body prepared. See that you eat nutritious food, get enough exercise and sleep well. Regular workouts help you to fight stress better, leading to better self-control. And the good news is, you don't have to spend hours in the gym every day. Even light exercise like taking a walk or doing basic yoga can enhance your resilience.

Make affirmations work for you

Self-affirmations can lead to better self-control. When your affirmations are positive and confident, and repeated often, they have a lasting impact on your mind. There's a world of difference between "I can't have that cheese pizza" as compared to "I don't want to have that cheese pizza". The former suggests your limitation while that latter indicates confidence.

Whenever you feel the need to boost your self-control, say these affirmations over and over again:

- I am in full control of myself.
- I am in full control of my reactions to external stimuli.
- I am in full control of my behavior.
- I am the master of my life.
- I possess the power to choose my thoughts and emotions.
- I understand that my self-control gives me inner strength.
- I am, with each passing day, enhancing my abilities to control myself.
- I practice self-control because it's a lot of fun.

Simple self-discipline workouts

There are several things in our everyday life that we refuse to do, purely because we lack the mental strength to do them. These could be small acts, seemingly insignificant, but with the potency to enhance our inner muscle and make us better individuals. We hesitate from doing them for a variety of reasons including laziness, low confidence and self-esteem, low mental strength, being shy and diffident or plain procrastination. A part of us may want to do it, but we vacillate and lose the opportunity, only to regret it later. This is where our mind plays a role in increasing our willpower.

- Your sink is full of dirty dishes and you're surfing the Internet mindlessly. Force yourself to reach for the Shut Down button, close the computer, and head towards the sink. Don't fall for any more procrastination. Start with cleaning just one spoon and soon you'll find yourself cleaning up the entire sink. It's your win against your sloth.

- A pregnant woman enters the subway carriage and no seat is empty. You have the choice to give her your seat but you hesitate. Don't. Do it for yourself, not for her or for the sake of being nice. Give her the seat and record a minor victory.

- You come back home from a tired day outdoors. You know you need to have a wash. But your mind tells you that you're fatigued beyond repair, so you just sit in front of the television watching senseless stuff. Don't believe yourself. Don't let yourself be taken for a ride. You do have the strength to walk into the shower and bathe. You'll feel so fresh that you'll be glad you did. More importantly, you would have triumphed over yourself.

Look around and you'll find dozens of similar instances where you're offered a choice – one, the usual easy route and the other, the unusual difficult one. Choose the difficult route always. Take the stairs instead of the elevator, walk instead of seeking a lift, hit the gym instead of sleeping early in the morning. Each such act of yours strengthens your willpower a little more. Become a strong personality, not a weakling at the mercy of your faint heart. Conquer yourself and you can vanquish the world.

SOLUTIONS SNAPSHOT
What we learnt in this chapter

Develop mental strength through willpower, self-control and discipline.

A strong willpower is behind self-control.

Willpower is like muscle; its strength can be enhanced through practice.

There are many benefits of willpower. It helps you become happy and successful.

Have the will to make willpower work. Here are some tips:

- Attempt to resist temptation at every step.
- If you can't say No right now, postpone yielding to temptation.
- Remove all enticements from around you. Out of sight, out of mind.
- Eat healthy food, get exercise, sleep well – all help fight temptation.
- Use self-affirmation to develop inner strength.
- Test your mental prowess during simple everyday events.
- You can't conquer the world if you fail to conquer yourself.

9 CONCLUSION

From sloth to super productivity

No one has ever drowned in sweat.

Lou Holtz

Okay, so we complete this journey here. In this trip, we've travelled from being lazy to being productive, from lacking in confidence to brimming with success.

Now you've all the tools, all the advice, all the paraphernalia required to take the leap. You know what comprises laziness, why you tend to be lazy and what you need to do to overcome it. You have every bit of information to defeat it and emerge the unopposed victor. Now what's your excuse?

While it's natural to feel lazy once in a while, when it becomes chronic is when you need to sit up and take notice. And yet there's a kind of laziness that comes upon you after a major assignment that lasts weeks. After it's done, signed and sealed, you feel being completely spent, not even capable of lifting a finger. This feeling could be classified as 'good' laziness and must be savored while it lasts. It's just a reward for all the hard work that you've put in.

But that sloth that is causeless, the idling of your engines with no reason – the 'bad' laziness – is what concerns us. This book is a treasure trove of ideas, guidance, and tips and tricks on how to overcome plain, raw laziness. And there's enough in here to stir the laziest person in the world to action. Go back to the advice, re-read them, soak yourself in the ideas, ingrain them in your mind. For quick recaps, read the small section called 'Solutions Snapshot' at the end of each chapter. It serves as your ready reckoner.

Finally we say good-bye. But not before wishing you unbridled success in your fight against that old bugbear that slows down the world: Laziness. It's been well said that no one has ever died of hard work. And you might reply that you don't want to be the first one to. But jokes aside, it's endeavor and enterprise that can propel you forward on the highway of life. So may you triumph in the big battles of the world, and may you live to change the universe! Adios!

ABOUT THE AUTHOR

Andrew Evans is an entrepreneur, motivational speaker, life coach with more than a decade's worth of experience.

His next step is making his expertise available to all the people who feel they are ready to face their bright future and become successful, however just need this tiniest final push. He considers his mission to convey to his readers the best ideas on how to improve yourself both personally and professionally. His approach to coaching is less fancy words - more easy to follow steps.

Made in the USA
San Bernardino, CA
18 March 2017